New Year 2023

Where Is My Home?

Where Is My Home?
Selected Short Poems of Rainer Maria Rilke
Translated from the German by Tilo Ulbricht

This edition has been published in 2023 in the United Kingdom
by Paper + Ink.

www.paperand.ink
Twitter: @paper_andink
Instagram: paper_and.ink

1 2 3 4 5 6 7 8 9 10

ISBN 9781911475651

English translation © Tilo Ulbricht, 2023
A CIP catalogue record for this book is available
from the British Library.

Jacket design by James Nunn: www.jamesnunn.co.uk | @Gnunkse

Printed and bound in Great Britain.

Where Is My Home?

SELECTED SHORT POEMS OF RAINER MARIA RILKE

TRANSLATED FROM THE GERMAN BY TILO ULBRICHT

Also by Tilo Ulbricht

Recollections: Trying to Follow a Way –
The Way of Questioning
(SomaHolis Publications, December 2022)

For Roy Ashwell
Poet and Friend

My sincere thanks to a friend who has patiently helped with the final revision of these poems, especially after an illness left my eyes even weaker than before.

Contents[1]

Introduction	11
1. Abend / Evening (1895)	18
2. Ich wollt, sie hätten statt der Wiege / I wish they hadn't made me a cradle (1896)	20
3. Ich weiß nicht, was mir geschieht ... / I don't know what is happening in me (1895)	22
4. Advent / Advent (1897)	24
5. Das ist mein Streit / This is my struggle (1897)	26
6. Warst du ein Kind ... / Where Is My Home? (1897)	28
7. Nennt ihr das Seele ... / What is chirping so ... (1897)	30
8. Ich lebe mein Leben in wachsenden Ringen / I live my life ... (1899)	32
9. Wenn es nur einmal so ganz stille wäre / If just once ... (1899)	34
10. Ich finde dich in allen diesen Dingen / I find you in all the things (1899)	36
11. Ihr vielen unbestürmten Städte / What of the enemy ... (1899)	38

---

1 Wherever Rilke gives a title to a poem, that title has been retained. For untitled poems, the first line (or part of it) is used, ending with an ellipsis. There is one exception: for poem no. 6, the last line is used as the title.

12. *Wie der Wächter in den Weingeländen /*
Like the Watchman in the Vineyards (1899) 40

13. *Gott spricht zu jedem nur ... /*
God only speaks to each one ... (1899) 42

14. *Du musst das Leben nicht verstehen /*
Don't tense to understand (1900) 44

15. *Schicksale sind ... / Destinies (1900)* 46

16. *Lösch mir die Augen aus ... /*
Quench my eyes ... (1901) 52

17. *Und doch, obwohl ein jeder von sich strebt /*
All Life Is Lived (1901) 54

18. *Die Könige der Welt sind alt /*
The rulers of this world are old (1901) 56

19. *Eingang / Entrance (1902)* 58

20. *Der Nachbar / The Neighbour (1902)* 60

21. *Einsamkeit / Loneliness (1902)* 62

22. *Herbsttag / Autumn Day (1902)* 64

23. *Herbst / Autumn (1902)* 66

24. *Die Städte aber wollen ... /*
Cities want everything ... (1903) 68

25. *Verkündigung – die Worte des Engels /*
Annunciation (1906) 70

26. *Der Schauende / In winter trees ... (1906)* 74

27. *Schlaflied / Lullaby (1906)* 78
28. *Wir* sind *ja ... / But we are ... (1906)* 80

29. *Liebes-lied / Love Song (1907)* 82

30. *Opfer / Sacrifice (1907)* 84

31. *Der Auszug des verlorenes Sohnes /*
The Departure of the Prodigal Son (1907)   86

32. *Abschied /* Parting (1907)   90

33. *Der Apfelgarten /* The Apple Orchard (1907,
Borgeby-Gård)   92

34. *Der Duft /* The Scent (1907–8)   94

35. *Das Rosen-Innere /* The Rose's Inner Space (1908)   96

36. *Die Liebende /* The Beloved (1908)   98

37. *Die Liebenden /* The Lovers (1908)   102

38. *Ich geh jetzt immer den gleichen Pfad /*
I always take the same path (1909)   104

39. *Von lauter Lauschen ... /*
From wonder and from listening ... (1909)   106

40. *Wenn die Uhren so nah /*
When the clocks strike (1909)   108

41. *Lange mußt du leiden ... /*
Long must you suffer ... (1913)   112

42. *Unwißend vor dem Himmel .../*
Unknowing in front of the Highest ... (1913)   114

43. *„Man muss sterben weil man sie kennt." /*
"One must die because one knows them." (1913)   116

44. *Es winkt zu Fühlung ... /*
All things beckon us to feel ... (1914)   120

45. *Ausgesetzt auf den Bergen des Herzens ... /*
Abandoned on the mountains of the heart (1914)   122

46. *Liebesanfang /* Love's Beginning (1915)   124

47. *Wunderliches Wort /* Strange saying (1919)   126

48. *O sage, Dichter ...* / Poet, tell us ... (1921) — 128

49. Die Sonette an Orpheus I–1: *Da stieg ein Baum ...*/The Sonnets to Orpheus I–1: There stands a tree ... (1922) — 130

50. Die Sonette an Orpheus II–27: *Gibt es wirklich ...* / The Sonnets to Orpheus II–27: Time the Destroyer (1922) — 132

51. *Sonett* / Sonnet — 134

52. *Imaginärer Lebenslauf* / An Imagined Life (1923) — 136

53. *Wir sind nur Mund* / Are we mute? (1923) — 138

54. *Schweigen* / Staying silent (1924) — 140

55. *Spaziergang* / My Walk (1924) — 142

56. *Eine Furche in meinem Hirn* / A furrow in my brain (1924) — 144

57. *Klang* / Sound (1925) — 146

58. *Rose, oh reiner Widerspruch* / Rose, oh pure contradiction ... (1925) — 148

59. *Bruder Körper ... / Brother body ... (1926)* — 150

60. *Komm du, du letzter ...* / Come, you last one ... (1926) — 152

61. Rilke's Walk with the Old Man: A Poem by the Translator — 155

Introduction

For many years I was an aspiring poet, long before I ever attempted any translation. One day, looking again at the poems I had 'written', it struck me that in almost all cases, I could remember the exact moment when the poem *came* to me.

We speak, in English, of *writing* poetry, but I no longer believe that a true poem is written; rather, it would be truer to say that the poet sometimes is able to *hear* a different, unusual sound – not ordinary 'thinking' – which can be given the form of a poem. It can then be written down, although in ancient times, poems were recited and passed on by word of mouth, such as *The Epic of Gilgamesh*.

But what is it the poet really *hears*? The poet may hear actual words, as Rainer Maria Rilke heard the opening lines of the "First Elegy" of *The Duino Elegies* whilst walking along the cliffs near the castle of Duino on the Adriatic. That sounds very romantic, but poems may be born anywhere: on top of a double-decker London bus; waiting for a train; walking in some grimy city street; or late at night, alone with a dark sky.

Is there, behind the world of appearances, an eternal, unchanging reality that I can sometimes feel? A nascent poem needs to be given form, so the poet – like any good craftsman – must have the skills needed, skills with words and rhythm. With the skills alone, no poem can appear. A poem is itself a translation, from the formless into a word-form.

Another way of saying this is that there are two languages. One underlies manifestation, and the other, in words, is *part* of manifestation. This is a very ancient idea, expressed in the Hindu Vedas. Poetry, at its highest, is a form of sacred literature, as the poet René Daumal affirmed.[2]

"The Departure of the Prodigal Son" was the first poem by Rilke that made a deep impression on me. When I first heard the parable itself, I had a very negative reaction to it. I felt that the son who left had been stupid to do so. How could he so completely forget, and waste, his father's inheritance? When he returned, why was he immediately forgiven?

Rilke threw a completely new light on the story. He does not retell the biblical version, he asks us to feel, to understand *why* the prodigal son left. How extraordinary! He *had* to leave: how can I find myself unless I first lose myself? I tried to translate that poem, but failed.

---

2 René Daumal, Rasa, *or Knowledge of the Self: Essays on Indian Aesthetics and Selected Sanskrit Studies*, translated by Louise Landes Levi, New York: New Directions, 1982.

I found that Rilke's first poems are conventional verses that do not prepare us for what came later. For example, here is the beginning of one of his early poems:

> I don't know what is happening in me,
> what bliss it is I'm longing for;
> my heart is taken in a dream,
> my longing is a song.

Many a young poet might have written verses such as these. A little later, there appears a poem in which one first hears a different voice – Rilke's first Rilkean poem:

> If you were a child in a happy flock
> you could not understand my hatred
> of the constant hostile danger
> that faced me every day.
> I felt an alien, abandoned like a stranger
> who only secretly sometimes could be content
> in a blossom-scented night in May.
>
> By day imprisoned by the tight ring
> of cowardly duty, devotedly performed;
> escaping in the evenings, not hearing
> the sound of a tiny window opening
> and a butterfly taking my longing
> on a silent voyage to ask the stars:
> *where is my home?*

This poem prepares us for "The Departure of the Prodigal Son":

> To go and leave all that confusion,
> what is ours and yet not really ours,
> the image mirrored in the fountain
> shattered when the water trembles;
> to leave all things which yet again
> cling to us like brambles –
> leave all this and that, already no longer
> seeing the so habitual and familiar, but then,
> seeing it again: a new beginning
> suddenly here ...

Rilke understood from his own experience that our state of consciousness varies. Moments of being, of clear perception, are rare and fleeting; in one moment we have a deep impression of reality, but in the next, we are lost again in 'thought'. Such changes of perception are the theme both of the *Elegies* and in the shorter poems I felt drawn to translate. This selection is thus very different from other published translations of Rilke's poetry.

*

Translating a poem into another language does not entail translating the *words*. The translator, guided by the words of the poem, needs to listen *inside*, to the sound from which the poem was born, and give it a form in a different language. To copy rhythm and rhyme from a different language makes no sense, because forms necessarily differ.

Human beings have two natures. Religious traditions speak of an earthly nature and a spiritual nature, corresponding to the two languages. This theme, expressed in metaphor, appears again and again in Rilke – for example, that each of us is akin to a besieged castle:

> What of the enemy, you unstormed cities?
> Have you never longed for him? Would he had
> besieged you
> through turbulent long years
> until, unconsoled and yet in sorrow
> and in hunger, you finally could bear him.
>
> Like fields and meadows, he is all around the city's
> walls ...

In one of Rilke's last poems, facing death at the end of his painful illness, there is a clear realisation that he is not his body:

> Brother body is poor ... so one must be rich for his
> sake.
> Often he was the rich one, so he may be forgiven

the poverty of his difficult moments.
If now he hardly seems to know us anymore,
one may gently remind him of all we have shared.

A note about *The Sonnets to Orpheus*

In 1922, a few years after completing *The Duino Elegies*, Rilke wrote *The Sonnets to Orpheus*, in two series totalling fifty-five poems. He adopted the Petrarchan form, which I am told can work well in Italian, but is very awkward in other languages. Reading these sonnets aloud, it is apparent that not only the vocabulary but also the word order and line breaks are determined not by the flow of the thought and feeling, but by the requirements of the form. Many are poor poems; one can make them scan by careful reading, but the impression is one of constraint. One is left wondering: what is it that Rilke is trying to express?

Although I have attempted translations of more than half of these sonnets, I am not satisfied that I have done them justice. In this selection, the very first along with one of the last are the only ones included. (The poem Rilke titled *"Sonett"*, which is also included, is not one of *The Sonnets to Orpheus*.)

A final note
One poem by the translator has been included at the end.

1. Abend (1895)

Der Abend wechselt langsam die Gewänder,
die ihm ein Rand von alten Bäumen hält;
du schaust: und von dir scheiden sich die Länder,
ein himmelfahrendes und eins, das fällt;

und lassen dich, zu keinem ganz gehörend,
nicht ganz so dunkel wie das Haus, das schweigt,
nicht ganz so sicher Ewiges beschwörend
wie das, was Stern wird jede Nacht und steigt –

und lassen dir (unsäglich zu entwirrn)
dein Leben bang und riesenhaft und reifend,
so daß es, bald begrenzt und bald begreifend,
abwechselnd Stein in dir wird und Gestirn.

1. Evening (1895)

As the evening slowly changes
the landscape held by that line of ancient trees,
you see your world divided into two – one rising
up to the heavens, the other falling back to Earth.

You are left not belonging quite to either,
neither as dark as that silent house, nor certain
like the star rising so confidently every night
that you have a place in the eternal.

Mysteriously, you are left not knowing,
your life unsure yet vast and growing.
It seems so limited – then suddenly goes far,
turning into something firm inside you, a gentle star.

2. Ich wollt, sie hätten statt der Wiege
   (1896)

Ich wollt, sie hätten statt der Wiege
mir einen kleinen Sarg gemacht,
dann war mir besser wohl, dann schwiege
die Lippe längst in feuchter Nacht.

Dann hätte nie ein wilder Wille
die bange Brust durchzittert, – dann
wärs in dem kleinen Körper stille,
so still wie's niemand denken kann.

Nur eine Kinderseele stiege
zum Himmel hoch so sacht, – ganz sacht ...
Was haben sie mir statt der Wiege
nicht einen kleinen Sarg gemacht?

2. I wish they hadn't made me a cradle
   (1896)

I wish they hadn't made me a cradle
but a little coffin.
I would feel better there, and already long ago
during long damp nights, my lips would have stayed still.

No wild urge would ever
have pierced my anxious breast,
which would be quiet in that little body,
even quieter than you can imagine.

There would just be a child's soul
rising so gently to Heaven ...
Why didn't they make me a coffin
in place of a cradle?

3. Ich weiß nicht, was mir geschieht ...
(1895)

Ich weiß nicht, wie mir geschieht ...
Weiß nicht, was Wonne ich lausche,
mein Herz ist fort wie im Rausche,
und die Sehnsucht ist wie ein Lied.

Und mein Mädel hat fröhliches Blut
und hat das Haar voller Sonne
und die Augen von der Madonne,
die heute noch Wunder tut.

3. I don't know what is happening in me
   (1895)

I don't know what is happening in me,
what bliss it is I'm longing for;
my heart is taken in a dream,
my longing is a song.

I feel there is joy in my girl's blood
and her hair is full of sun,
her eyes, the eyes of the Madonna,
bringing miracles to life.

4. Advent (1897)

Es treibt der Wind im Winterwalde
Die Flockenherde wie ein Hirt,
Und manche Tanne ahnt, wie balde
Sie fromm und lichterheilig wird,
Und lauscht hinaus. Den weißen Wegen
Streckt sie die Zweige hin – bereit,
Und wehrt dem Wind und wächst entgegen
Der einen Nacht der Herrlichkeit.

4. Advent (1897)

Like a shepherd, the wind is driving
snowflakes through the winter woods;
there is one fir tree, which feels that soon
it will be standing very still,
holy with light. Listening,
stretching its arms to the white of the footpath
and resolute against the wind, it is growing
in readiness for one night of splendour.

5. Das ist mein Streit (1897)

Das ist mein Streit:
Sehnsuchtsgeweiht
durch alle Tage schweifen.
Dann, stark und breit,
mit tausend Wurzelstreifen
tief in das Leben greifen –
und durch das Leid
weit aus dem Leben reifen,
weit aus der Zeit!

5. This is my struggle (1897)

This is my struggle:
initiated by longing
to wander through all my days until,
widened and made strong,
I reach deep into life with a thousand roots,
and through suffering
beyond time.

6. Warst du ein Kind ... (1897)

Warst du ein Kind in froher Schar,
dann kannst du's freilich nicht erfassen,
wie es mir kam, den Tag zu hassen
als ewig feindliche Gefahr.
Ich war so fremd und so verlassen,
daß ich nur tief in blütenblassen
Mainächten heimlich selig war.

Am Tag trug ich den engen Ring
der feigen Pflicht in frommer Weise.
Doch abends schlich ich aus dem Kreise,
mein kleines Fenster klirrte – kling –
sie wußtens nicht. Ein Schmetterling,
nahm meine Sehnsucht ihre Reise,
weil sie die weiten Sterne leise
nach ihrer Heimat fragen ging.

6. Where Is My Home? (1897)

If you were a child in a happy flock
you could not understand my hatred
of the constant hostile danger
that faced me every day.
I felt an alien, abandoned like a stranger
who only secretly sometimes could be content
in a blossom-scented night in May.

By day imprisoned by the tight ring
of cowardly duty, devotedly performed;
escaping in the evenings, not hearing
the sound of a tiny window opening
and a butterfly taking my longing
on a silent voyage to ask the stars:
where is my home?

7. Nennt ihr das Seele ... (1897)

Nennt ihr das Seele, was so zage zirpt
in euch? Was, wie der Klang der Narrenschellen,
um Beifall bettelt und um Würde wirbt,
und endlich arm ein armes Sterben stirbt
im Weihrauchabend gotischer Kapellen, –
nennt ihr das Seele?

Schau ich die blaue Nacht, vom Mai verschneit,
in der die Welten weite Wege reisen,
mir ist: ich trage ein Stück Ewigkeit
in meiner Brust. Das rüttelt und das schreit
und will hinauf und will mir ihnen kreisen ...
Und das ist Seele.

7. What is chirping so ... (1897)

What is chirping so timidly in you –
do you call that soul? The bells of a madcap fool
who is begging for approval and dignity, ring like that,
but in the end he's poor, and so is his death
in some incense-laden gothic chapel –
do you call that soul?

When I see how May has speckled her blue night
with shining sparks of snow, the stars
travelling their far roads alone,
I feel within my breast
a fragment of eternity. It moves and cries,
it longs to rise up and circle with them, to be whole –
that is soul.

8. Ich lebe mein Leben in wachsenden Ringen (1899)

Ich lebe mein Leben in wachsenden Ringen,
die sich über die Dinge ziehn.
Ich werde den letzten vielleicht nicht vollbringen,
aber versuchen will ich ihn.

Ich kreise um Gott, um den uralten Turm,
und ich kreise jahrtausendelang;
und ich weiß noch nicht: bin ich ein Falke, ein Sturm
oder ein großer Gesang.

8. I live my life ... (1899)

I live my life in widening circles
That stretch to encompass all things.
I may not reach to the very last,
but attempt it I shall.

I circle around God, around the ancient tower,
I circle for a thousand years;
and still I do not know –
am I a falcon,
am I wind become storm,
or am I a great song?

9. Wenn es nur einmal so ganz stille wäre (1899)

Wenn es nur einmal so ganz stille wäre.
Wenn das Zufällige und Ungefähre
verstummte und das nachbarliche Lachen,
wenn das Geräusch, das meine Sinne machen,
mich nicht so sehr verhinderte am Wachen –:

Dann könnte ich in einem tausendfachen
Gedanken bis an deinen Rand dich denken

und dich besitzen (nur ein Lächeln lang),
um dich an alles Leben zu verschenken
wie einen Dank.

9. If just once ... (1899)

If just once, everything was completely still,
if chance events and actions that miss their mark
fell silent, and the next-door laughter
and the noises from my own restlessness
did not so hinder me from being alert ...

Then in one far-reaching movement
my thought could find you
in the place where you begin,
and completely hold you
(but no longer than a smile),
and let go in gratitude, to give you,
freely give you to all of life.

10. Ich finde dich in allen diesen Dingen
   (1899)

Ich finde dich in allen diesen Dingen,
denen ich gut und wie ein Bruder bin;
als Samen sonnst du dich in den geringen
und in den großen giebst du groß dich hin.

Das ist das wundersame Spiel der Kräfte,
dass sie so dienend durch die Dinge gehn:
in Wurzeln wachsend, schwindend in die Schäfte
und in den Wipfeln wie ein Auferstehn.

10. I find you in all the things (1899)

I find you in all the things
to which I feel related like a brother;
as a seed you sun yourself in what is small,
and in bounty give yourself to what is great.

This is the mysterious world of forces
That act in and through all things –
growing in roots, waning in the rising trunks
and in the crown, to be reborn.

11. Ihr vielen unbestürmten Städte (1899)

Ihr vielen unbestürmten Städte,
habt ihr euch nie den Feind ersehnt?
O dass er euch belagert hätte
ein langes schwankendes Jahrzehnt.

Bis ihr ihn trostlos und in Trauern,
bis dass ihr hungernd ihn ertrugt;
er liegt wie Landschaft vor den Mauern,
denn also weiß er auszudauern
um jene, die er heimgesucht.

Schaut aus vom Rande eurer Dächer
da lagert er und wird nicht matt
und wird nicht weniger und schwächer

und schickt nicht Droher und Versprecher
und Überreder in die Stadt.

Er ist der große Mauerbrecher,
der eine stumme Arbeit hat.

11. **What of the enemy ...** (1899)

What of the enemy, you unstormed cities?
Have you never longed for him?
Would he had besieged you
through turbulent long years
until, unconsoled and yet in sorrow
and in hunger, you finally could bear him.

Like fields and meadows, he is all around the city's walls
lying in wait for those whom he pursues;
for enduring, he knows well.

From your rooftops now, look out:
there he is encamped; he does not tire
and is not less or weaker than he was,
yet to the city sends neither promises nor threats.

His is a silent work, that great
breaker-down of walls.

12. Wie der Wächter in den Weingeländen
   (1899)

Wie der Wächter in den Weingeländen
seine Hütte hat und wacht,
bin ich Hütte, Herr, in deinen Händen
und bin Nacht, o Herr, von deiner Nacht.

Weinberg, Weide, alter Apfelgarten,
Acker, der kein Frühjahr überschlägt,
Feigenbaum, der auch im marmorharten
Grunde hundert Früchte trägt:

Duft geht aus aus deinen runden Zweigen.
Und du fragst nicht, ob ich wachsam sei;
furchtlos, aufgelöst in Säften, steigen
deine Tiefen still an mir vorbei.

12. Like the Watchman in the Vineyards
(1899)

In the vineyard there is a watchman,
and a hut. In your hands, oh Lord,
am I a watchman, or just a hut?
Am I a night in your great night?

Vineyard, meadow, apple orchard,
field which no Spring can overlook,
and even in ground as hard as marble,
fig tree, you bear a hundred fruits;

there are scents from your rounded boughs,
and something rises fearlessly into the sap;
without insisting that I am watchful,
silently, it passes by.

13. Gott spricht zu jedem nur ... (1899)

Gott spricht zu jedem nur, eh er ihn macht,
dann geht er schweigend mit ihm aus der Nacht.
Aber die Worte, eh jeder beginnt,
diese wolkigen Worte, sind:

Von deinen Sinnen hinausgesandt,
geh bis an deiner Sehnsucht Rand;
gieb mir Gewand.

Hinter den Dingen wachse als Brand,
dass ihre Schatten, ausgespannt,
immer mich ganz bedecken.

Lass dir Alles geschehn: Schönheit und Schrecken.
Man muss nur gehn: Kein Gefühl ist das fernste.
Lass dich von mir nicht trennen.
Nah ist das Land,
das sie das Leben nennen.

Du wirst es erkennen
an seinem Ernste.

Gieb mir die Hand.

13. God only speaks to each one ... (1899)

God only speaks to each one before creating him,
then silently goes with him out of the night.
These are the strange words spoken
before each one of us begins:

Sent out from your senses,
go to the limits of your longing;
clothe Me.

Grow like a fire behind the forms
so that their shadows spread out
and cover Me entirely.

Let all things come to pass, both beauty and terror,
for one must go on; no feeling is farthest.
Do not let yourself be parted from Me.
The land they call life is
here, close by.

You will recognise it;
it is serious.

Give Me your hand.

14. Du musst das Leben nicht verstehen
(1900)

Du musst das Leben nicht verstehen,
dann wird es werden wie ein Fest.
Und lass dir jeden Tag geschehen
so wie ein Kind im Weitergehen von jedem Wehen
sich viele Blüten schenken lässt.

Sie aufzusammeln und zu sparen,
das kommt dem Kind nicht in den Sinn.
Es löst sie leise aus den Haaren,
drin sie so gern gefangen waren,
und hält den lieben jungen Jahren
nach neuen seine Hände hin.

14 . **Don't tense to understand** (1900)

Don't tense to understand,
and life becomes a celebration.
Let every day just come to you
as to a child, who in walking on,
accepts from every sorrow
the gift of many blossoms.

A child would never think
to collect and save them,
but gently tease them out of its hair
to which they like to cling,
and will hold out its hands anew
to whatever fresh years may bring.

15. Schicksale sind ... (1900)

Für Heinrich Vogeler

Schicksale sind (ich fühl es alle Tage)
viel mehr als Zufall, weniger als Lose.
Sind – Luft, gefühlt von einem Flügelschlage,
Abende im Bewußtsein einer Rose.
Und alles Tägliche und Unbetonte
ist Schicksal, wenn es einem ganz geschieht, –
und Schicksal ist ein jedes Lied,
wenn es im Schweigen jener sich belohnte,
die es umzieht...

Es kommt nur auf das eine Wachsen an
über die allertiefsten Dinge,
nur so zu werden, daß man das Geringe
mit seinen Sinnen nicht mehr finden kann.
Und so zu sinnen, als ob keiner sann,
und so zu gehen, als ob keiner ginge ...

Denn wirklich ist noch nie etwas erlebt,
von allem wesenhaften Wunderbaren, –
vor deinen Türen steht der Tag und bebt,
und seine wachsende Gebärde strebt
nach deinen Sinnen, um sich zu erfahren.
Nim etwas auf und sei es irgendwas:

15. Destinies (1900)

For Heinrich Vogeler

Every day I feel destinies to be
more than mere coincidence, yet less than fate.
They are sensed like the air from the beat of a wing,
like evenings in the awareness of a rose;
all everyday undramatised events
are destiny, when accepted fully. Destiny is song,
when someone allows himself to be included
and in silence is able to receive it.

All depends on such a growing through
the deepest, deepest things,
in order to be such
that with one's senses one is no longer caught
by what is low and small,
and so to ponder as though there were
no thinker, and to walk
as if no one were walking.

For nothing has yet truly been lived through,
all that which in itself is wonder-full. Look,
the day stands trembling before your door,
its opening embrace reaching
towards your senses, to know itself in you.

war Liebe einmal schon gelebt gewesen?
und war schon einmal einer auserlesen
zu einem übergroßen Haß?
Das kam wohl alles über den und jenen –
aber nicht ganz, ohne Zusammenhang.
Wir wollen uns nach aller Ganzheit sehnen:
wir wollen Klang.

Alles Gefühl, in Gestalten und Handlungen
wird es unendlich groß und leicht.
Ich ruhe nicht, bis ich das eine erreicht:
Bilder zu finden für meine Verwandlungen.
Mir genügt nicht das steigende Lied.
Einmal muß ich es mächtig wagen,
weithin sichtbar auszusagen
was im Ahnen kaum geschieht.

Just take up something, whatever it might be:
was love ever really lived – even once?
And was someone chosen once
for a massive hatred?
To one or another it all came to pass,
but incompletely, without relation.
It is wholeness we now long for –
we long for it to resonate in us.

All feeling can become infinitely large
and light in its action, in its forms.
I shall not rest until I succeed in finding
what I must find: images for transformation.
For me a song rising up is not enough-
I must dare just once
to bear witness, openly,
to what I have barely perceived,
to what hardly seems to have taken place.

Alternative translation of the second stanza:

Now there is nothing but to grow
through and then beyond
the deepest, deepest things,
in order to become, to be,
so that the least of things
no more my senses catch,
and to find that silent thought
in which no thinker is,
so to manifest
no person.

16. Lösch mir die Augen aus ... (1901)

Lösch mir die Augen aus: ich kann dich sehn,
wirf mir die Ohren zu: ich kann dich hören,
und ohne Füße kann ich zu dir gehn,
und ohne Mund noch kann ich dich beschwören.
Brich mir die Arme ab, ich fasse dich
mit meinem Herzen wie mit einer Hand,
halt mir das Herz zu, und mein Hirn wird schlagen,
und wirfst du in mein Hirn den Brand,
so werd ich dich auf meinem Blute tragen.

16. Quench my eyes ... (1901)

Quench my eyes, I still can see you;
seal my ears, I still can hear you;
without feet, I still can find you;
without lips, I can yet evoke you;
break off my arms, I will hold you
with my heart as with a hand;
hold it shut, my brain will call you –
thrust into it a burning brand,
I yet will carry you,
in my singing blood.

17. Und doch, obwohl ein jeder von sich strebt (1901)

Und doch, obwohl ein jeder von sich strebt
wie aus dem Kerker, der ihn hasst und hält, -
es ist ein großes Wunder in der Welt:
ich fühle: alles Leben wird gelebt.

Wer lebt es denn? Sind das die Dinge, die
wie eine ungespielte Melodie
im Abend wie in einer Harfe stehn?
Sind das die Winde, die von Wassern wehn,
sind das die Zweige, die sich Zeichen geben,
sind das die Blumen, die die Düfte weben,
sind das die langen alternden Alleen?
Sind das die warmen Tiere, welche gehn,
sind das die Vögel, die sich fremd erheben?

Wer lebt es denn? Lebst du es, Gott, – das Leben?

17. All Life Is Lived (1901)

Each one of us is struggling
inside a dungeon that hates and holds us;
yet I feel a great wonder in this world:
all life is lived.

Who lives it, then? Is it all the things
that, at evening, mutely stand
like unplayed melodies on a harp?
Is it the winds, blown by the oceans,
is it the branches gesturing to their neighbours,
is it the flowers weaving their scents,
is it the long tree-lined avenues growing older,
is it the animals welcoming the morning,
is it the birds, rising up like strangers?

Who is living ... everything? Are you living it, God?
Is it you ... living life?

18. Die Könige der Welt sind alt (1901)

Die Könige der Welt sind alt
und werden keine Erben haben.
Die Söhne sterben schon als Knaben,
und ihre bleichen Töchter gaben
die kranken Kronen der Gewalt.

Der Pöbel bricht sie klein zu Geld,
der zeitgemäße Herr der Welt
dehnt sie im Feuer zu Maschinen,
die seinem Wollen grollend dienen;
aber das Glück ist nicht mit ihnen.

Das Erz hat Heimweh. Und verlassen
will es die Münzen und die Räder,
die es ein kleines Leben lehren.
Und aus Fabriken und aus Kassen
wird es zurück in das Geäder
der aufgetanen Berge kehren,
die sich verschließen hinter ihm.

18. The rulers of this world are old (1901)

The rulers of this world are old;
they shall have no heirs; just boys,
their sons, already dying,
and their pale daughters give up
their power to the sick.

The rabble breaks them down to coins,
and in furnaces the lord of this world
will turn them into machines
which sullenly obey his will;
good fortune will not befall them.

The ore longs for home,
to abandon coins and wheels
which teach it a mean constricted life.
From factories and the tills of cash
it longs to return to the veins
of the plundered mountains,
which will shut behind it.

19. Eingang (1902)

Wer du auch seist: am Abend tritt hinaus
aus deiner Stube, drin du alles weißt;
als letztes vor der Ferne liegt dein Haus:
wer du auch seist.

Mit deinen Augen, welche müde kaum
von der verbrauchten Schwelle sich befrein,
hebst du ganz langsam einen schwarzen Baum
und stellst ihn vor den Himmel: schlank, allein.
Und hast die Welt gemacht. Und sie ist groß
und wie ein Wort, das noch im Schweigen reift.
Und wie dein Wille ihren Sinn begreift,
lassen sie deine Augen zärtlich los ...

19. Entrance (1902)

Whoever you may be, leave your room at evening,
leave everything you seem to know –
your house, the last before the very end:
whoever you may be.

Your tired eyes can hardly free themselves
from the worn-out threshold of your door,
but slowly they can lift
one black tree against the heavens,
slender and alone, and so create the world.
It is great, a spoken word
growing into silence, and as you grasp its meaning
it gently loosens its hold on you.

20. Der Nachbar (1902)

Fremde Geige, gehst du mir nach?
In wieviel fernen Städten schon sprach
deine einsame Nacht zu meiner?
Spielen dich hunderte? Spielt dich einer?

Giebt es in allen großen Städten
solche, die sich ohne dich
schon in den Flüssen verloren hätten?
Und warum trifft es immer mich?

Warum bin ich immer der Nachbar derer,
die dich bange zwingen zu singen
und zu sagen: Das Leben ist schwerer
als die Schwere von allen Dingen.

20. The Neighbour (1902)

Unknown violin, are you following me?
In how many distant cities has your lonely night
already spoken to mine?
Are hundreds playing you ... or only one?

In the great cities, are there
some, not having heard your sound,
who would have lost themselves in the rivers?
Why is it always I who am struck by this?

Why do I feel close to those
who make you sing
that life is harder and heavier
than the weight of everything?

21. Einsamkeit (1902)

Die Einsamkeit ist wie ein Regen.
Sie steigt vom Meer den Abenden entgegen;
von Ebenen, die fern sind und entlegen,
geht sie zum Himmel, der sie immer hat.
Und erst vom Himmel fällt sie auf die Stadt.

Regnet hernieder in den Zwitterstunden,
wenn sich nach Morgen wenden alle Gassen
und wenn die Leiber, welche nichts gefunden,
enttäuscht und traurig von einander lassen;
und wenn die Menschen, die einander hassen,
in einem Bett zusammen schlafen müssen:

dann geht die Einsamkeit mit den Flüssen ...

21. Loneliness (1902)

Loneliness is like the rain that rises from the sea
to meet the evening;
it rises from remote far plains to the heavens
that have always held it,
and only then falls on the city.

The rain falls in the in-between hours when
all alleys turn towards morning,
and bodies, having found nothing,
turn away sad and disappointed,
and some who hate each other
must share the same bed.

Loneliness flows in the rivers ...

22. Herbsttag (1902)

Herr: es ist Zeit. Der Sommer war sehr groß.
Leg deinen Schatten auf die Sonnenuhren,
und auf den Fluren laß die Winde los.

Befiehl den letzten Früchten voll zu sein;
gieb ihnen noch zwei südlichere Tage,
dränge sie zur Vollendung hin und jage
die letzte Süße in den schweren Wein.

Wer jetzt kein Haus hat, baut sich keines mehr.
Wer jetzt allein ist, wird es lange bleiben,
wird wachen, lesen, lange Briefe schreiben
und wird in den Alleen hin und her
unruhig wandern, wenn die Blätter treiben.

22. **Autumn Day** (1902)

Lord, it is time. The summer was great.
Now let fall your shadow on the sundials,
and across the hallways let loose the winds.

Command the last fruits now to ripen:
give them two more warm days from the south,
drive them to completion and chase
the final sweetness into heavy wine.

Who has no house will not build now.
Who is alone, alone shall stay,
will wake and read, write long letters
and in the avenues, here and there, wander
restless where the leaves are blown.

23. Herbst (1902)

Die Blätter fallen, fallen wie von weit,
als welkten in den Himmeln ferne Gärten;
sie fallen mit verneinender Gebärde.

Und in den Nächten fällt die schwere Erde
aus allen Sternen in die Einsamkeit.

Wir alle fallen. Diese Hand da fällt.
Und sieh dir andre an: Es ist in allen.

Und doch ist einer, welcher dieses Fallen
unendlich sanft in seinen Händen hält.

23. Autumn (1902)

The leaves are falling as from afar,
as though in distant gardens in the heavens
the trees were turning in a gesture of denial.

And in the nights, the heavy Earth
falls from the stars and finds itself alone.

We all are falling; this hand too is falling;
and look: the others too, it is in all of us.

Yet there is one who, with infinite gentleness
holds in his hands this falling.

24. Die Städte aber wollen ... (1903)

Die Städte aber wollen nur das ihre
und reißen alles mit in ihren Lauf.
Wie hohles Holz zerbrechen sie die Tiere
und brauchen viele Völker brennend auf.

Und ihre Menschen dienen in Kulturen
und fallen tief aus Gleichgewicht und Maß,
und nennen Fortschritt ihre Schneckenspuren
und fahren rascher, wo sie langsam fuhren,
und fühlen sich und funkeln wie die Huren
und lärmen lauter mit Metall und Glas.

Es ist, als ob ein Trug sie täglich äffte,
sie können gar nicht mehr sie selber sein;
das Geld wächst an, hat alle ihre Kräfte
und ist wie Ostwind groß, und sie sind klein
und ausgeholt und warten, daß der Wein
und alles Gift der Tier- und Menschensäfte
sie reize zu vergänglichem Geschäfte.

24. Cities want everything ... (1903)

Cities want everything only for themselves,
and on their way, tear down what's in front of them,
breaking animals like bits of hollowed wood,
consuming human beings in the fire.

Their inhabitants serve them blindly, falling completely
out of balance and all restraint.
Their snails' tracks they call progress,
going faster now, where more slowly went before,
and feel themselves like glittering whores,
noisier yet with metal and with glass.

Every day they are deceived again, for just like apes
they can no longer be themselves at all;
money has all their strength and keeps increasing
like a great wind from the East
but they are small,
made hollow, waiting for wine and poison
from all animal and human life
to seduce them to a meaningless existence.

25. Verkündigung – die Worte des Engels
(1906)

Du bist nicht näher an Gott als wir;
wir sind ihm alle weit.
Aber wunderbar sind dir
die Hände benedeit.
So reifen sie bei keiner Frau,
so schimmernd aus dem Saum:
ich bin der Tag, ich bin der Tau,
du aber bist der Baum.

Ich bin jetzt matt, mein Weg war weit,
vergieb mir, ich vergaß,
was Er, der groß in Goldgeschmeid
wie in der Sonne saß,
dir künden ließ, du Sinnende,
(verwirrt hat mich der Raum).
Sieh: ich bin das Beginnende,
du aber bist der Baum.

Ich spannte meine Schwingen aus
und wurde seltsam weit;
jetzt überfließt dein kleines Haus
von meinem großen Kleid.

25. Annunciation (1906)

You are not nearer God than we;
from Him are we all far.
Your hands are uniquely blessed;
wonderful how they emerge
radiantly from their sleeves,
prepared as no other woman's are.
I am the day, I am the dew,
but thou, thou art the tree.

I am exhausted now, having come so far;
by space I am left bewildered,
forgive me my forgetting
what He, seated in the sun
and great in His gold array
asked me to tell you, quiet one.
I am the one unique beginning,
but thou, thou art the tree.

I spread out my wings
becoming strangely wide
and your little house quite overflows
with my generous robes.

Und dennoch bist du so allein
wie nie und schaust mich kaum;
das macht: ich bin ein Hauch im Hain,
du aber bist der Baum.

Die Engel alle bangen so,
lassen einander los:
noch nie war das Verlangen so, so
ungewiss und groß.
Vielleicht, dass Etwas bald geschieht,
das du im Traum begreifst.
Gegrüßt sei, meine Seele sieht:
du bist bereit und reifst.
Du bist ein großes, hohes Tor,
und aufgehn wirst du bald.
Du, meines Liedes liebstes Ohr,
jetzt fühle ich: mein Wort verlor
sich in dir wie im Wald.

So kam ich und vollendete
dir tausendeinen Traum.
Gott sah mich an; er blendete...

Du aber bist der Baum.

Now you are more alone than ever
and hardly look at me;
I am just a breath in the wood.
but thou, thou art the tree.

Fearful and trembling
the angels let each other go;
never was there a longing
so great and so unknown.
Something may happen soon,
you will know it in a dream.
I greet you, for my soul can see
you are prepared and ripening.
You are a great, high gate
and will open soon.
You are my song's best-loved ear,
the forest in which my word is lost.

So it is I came to fulfil
your ultimate, thousandth dream.
God looked and dazzled me ...

But thou, thou art the tree.

26. Der Schauende (1906)

Ich sehe den Bäumen die Stürme an,
die aus laugewordenen Tagen
an meine ängstlichen Fenster schlagen,
und höre die Fernen Dinge sagen,
die ich nicht ohne Freund ertragen,
nicht ohne Schwester lieben kann.

Da geht der Sturm, ein Umgestalter,
geht durch den Wald und durch die Zeit,
und alles ist wie ohne Alter:
die Landschaft, wie ein Vers im Psalter,
ist Ernst und Wucht und Ewigkeit.

Wie ist das klein, womit wir ringen,
was mit uns ringt, wie ist das groß;
ließen wir, ähnlicher den Dingen,
uns so vom großen Sturm bezwingen, -
wir würden weit und namenlos.

Was wir besiegen, ist das Kleine,
und der Erfolg selbst macht uns klein.
Das Ewige und Ungemeine
will nicht von uns gebogen sein.

26. In winter trees ... (1906)

In winter trees on lukewarm days
I see the imprint of the storms
that beat on my anxious windows.
I then can hear what distant things are saying,
but without a friend I cannot bear it,
without a sister, I cannot love.

The formless storm drives on
through forest and through time,
as though everything were ageless,
and the landscape spoke truly like the psalm,
of what is really serious, of power,
of that which is beyond time.

How small, the things we wrestle with,
how great, what is wrestling with us;
if we could submit to that great storm
in the way that all things submit, to give us form,
we then would grow to be, not needing any name.

What we can defeat is small,
but the eternal and extraordinary
refuse to be ruled by us.

Das ist der Engel, der den Ringern
des Alten Testaments erschien:
wenn seiner Widersacher Sehnen
im Kampfe sich metallen dehnen,
fühlt er sie unter seinen Fingern
wie Saiten tiefer Melodien.

Wen dieser Engel überwand,
welcher so oft auf Kampf verzichtet,
der geht gerecht und aufgerichtet
und groß aus jener harten Hand,
die sich, wie formend, an ihn schmiegte.
Die Siege laden ihn nicht ein.
Sein Wachstum ist: der Tiefbesiegte
von immer Größerem zu sein.

This is the angel who appeared
to the wrestler in the Bible,
when the opponent's sinews
stretch like metal in the fight,
his fingers sensing them like strings,
played a deeper melody.

Conquered by that angel –
who could let go of any fight –
he emerged straight and tall to walk erect,
intimately moulded by that firm hand.
Victories did not beguile him:
it is from always being vanquished
by what is greater, that he grows.

27. Schlaflied (1906)

Einmal wenn ich dich verlier,
wirst du schlafen können, ohne
dass ich wie eine Lindenkrone
mich verflüstre über dir?

Ohne dass ich hier wache und
Worte, beinah wie Augenlider,
auf deine Brüste, auf deine Glieder
niederlege, auf deinen Mund.

Ohne dass ich dich verschließ
und dich allein mit Deinem lasse
wie einen Garten mit einer Masse
von Melissen und Stern-Anis.

27. Lullaby (1906)

One day I shall lose you.
Will you be able to sleep
when I am not there to whisper over you,
like the crown of a linden tree,

and I, watching,
can I lay my words – almost like eyelids –
here, on your breasts,
on your limbs and on your mouth,
without shutting you away ?

I must leave you with what is your own,
like a scented garden filled with lemon balm and star
anise.

28. Wir *sind* ja...

An die Prinzessin M. von B.

Wir *sind* ja. Doch kaum anders als den Lämmern
gehn uns die Tage hin mit Flucht und Schein;
auch uns verlangt, sooft die Wiesen dämmern,
zurückzugehn. Doch treibt uns keiner ein.

Wir bleiben draußen Tag und Nacht und Tag.
Die Sonne tut uns wohl, uns schreckt der Regen;
wir dürfen aufstehn und uns niederlegen
und etwas mutig sein und etwas zag.

Nur manchmal, während wir so schmerzhaft reifen,
daß wir an diesem beinah sterben, dann:
formt sich aus allem, was wir nicht begreifen,
ein Angesicht und sieht uns strahlend an.

28. But we *are*...

To Princess M. von B.

But we *are* – yet hardly different from lambs;
days pass us by, lost in flight and in appearances;
like them, when twilight returns to our meadow,
we long to go back – but no one drives us home.

Day and night and day we stay outside:
in the sun we feel well, frightened by the rain;
allowed to get up, to lie down,
now timid, now feeling some courage.

Just sometimes while we grow so painfully
that in this doing we almost die, then
there is formed from all we do but do not understand,
a face: it looks at us and shines.

29. Liebes-lied (1907)

Wie soll ich meine Seele halten, daß
sie nicht an deine rührt? Wie soll ich sie
hinheben über dich zu andern Dingen?
Ach gerne möcht ich sie bei irgendwas
Verlorenem im Dunkeln unterbringen
an einer fremden stillen Stelle, die
nicht weiterschwingt, wenn deine Tiefen schwingen.
Doch alles, was uns anrührt, dich und mich,
nimmt uns zusammen wie ein Bogenstrich,
der aus zwei Saiten eine Stimme zieht.
Auf welches Intrument sind wir gespannt?
Und welcher Geiger hat uns in der Hand?
O süßes Lied.

29. Love Song (1907)

How shall I hold my soul
so as not to intrude on yours? How shall I lift it
above and beyond you, to other things?
I wish to put it in the dark,
near something lost, in a far, still place
which will not resonate
when you vibrate deep down.
Yet everything which touches us, you and I,
brings us together, like the bow of a violin
drawing one note from two strings.
On what instrument are we played?
What musician has us in his hand?
Oh, sweet song.

30. Opfer (1907)

O wie blüht mein Leib aus jeder Ader
duftender seitdem ich dich erkenn;
sieh, ich gehe schlanker und gerader,
und du wartest nur –: wer bist du denn?

Sieh: ich fühle wie ich mich entferne,
wie ich Altes, Blatt um Blatt, verlier.
Nur dein Lächeln steht wie lauter Sterne
über dir und bald auch über mir.

Alles was durch meine Kinderjahre
namenlos noch und wie Wasser glänzt
will ich nach dir nennen am Altare,
der entzündet ist von deinem Haare
und mit deinen Brüsten leicht bekränzt.

30. Sacrifice (1907)

Since that shock of recognition, how my flesh
is flowering, more scented now in every vein.
See how I am walking: more slim, more straight.
And you, just waiting … Who *are* you?

See: I feel that as I left you,
I lost all that's old, leaf by leaf.
Only your smile stands over you
like the stars, and soon will be over me.

Everything that was still nameless in my childhood
yet shone through it like a stream.
At the altar I shall name it after you,
ignited by your hair,
and gently crowned with your breasts.

31. Der Auszug des verlorenes Sohnes
(1907)

Nun fortzugehn von alle dem Verworrnen,
das unser ist und uns doch nicht gehört,
das, wie das Wasser in den alten Bornen,
uns zitternd spiegelt und das Bild zerstört;
von allem diesen, das sich wie mit Dornen
noch einmal an uns anhängt – fortzugehn
und Das und Den,
die man schon nicht mehr sah
(so täglich waren sie und so gewöhnlich),
auf einmal anzuschauen: sanft, versöhnlich
und wie an einem Anfang und von nah
und ahnend einzusehn, wie unpersönlich,
wie über alle hin das Leid geschah,
von dem die Kindheit voll war bis zum Rand –:
Und dann doch fortzugehen, Hand aus Hand,
als ob man ein Geheiltes neu zerrisse,
und fortzugehn: wohin? Ins Ungewisse,
weit in ein unverwandtes warmes Land,
das hinter allem Handeln wie Kulisse
gleichgültig sein wird: Garten oder Wand;
und fortzugehn: warum? Aus Drang, aus Artung,
aus Ungeduld, aus dunkeler Erwartung,

31. The Departure of the Prodigal Son
(1907)

To go and leave all that confusion,
what is ours and yet not really ours,
the image mirrored in the fountain
shatters when the water trembles;
to leave all things that yet again
cling to us like brambles –
leave all this and that, already no longer
seeing the so habitual and familiar, but then,
seeing it again: a new beginning
suddenly here, gentle and accepting, very near;
sensing how grief impartially all things befell,
filling childhood to the very brim –
and yet, to go, wrenching hand from hand,
once more tearing at that which had been healed;
to depart: whereto? Into the unknown,
far into a warm but foreign land
as indifferent as a backdrop behind events:
here, a garden, there, a wall;
to go: why? To go into the dark,
from some impulse

aus Unverständlichkeit und Unverstand:
Dies alles auf sich nehmen und vergebens
vielleicht Gehaltnes fallen lassen, um
allein zu sterben, wissend nicht warum –

Ist das der Eingang eines neuen Lebens?

neither understanding nor understood,
impatient and expectant ...
To take all this upon oneself, let fall –
in vain perhaps – what had been held,
in order to die alone, not knowing why ...

Is this the doorway to another life?

32. Abschied (1907)

Wie hab ich das gefühlt, was Abschied heißt.
Wie weiß ich's noch: ein dunkles unverwundnes
Grausames Etwas, das ein Schönverbundnes
Noch einmal zeigt und hinhält und zerreißt.

Wie war ich ohne Wehr, dem zuzuschauen,
Das, da es mich, mich rufend, gehen ließ,
Zurückblieb, so als wären's alle Frauen
Und dennoch klein und weiß und nichts als dies:

Ein Winken, schon nicht mehr auf mich bezogen,
Ein leise Weiterwinkendes –, schon kaum
Erklärbar mehr: vielleicht ein Pflaumenbaum,
Von dem ein Kuckuck hastig abgeflogen.

32. Parting (1907)

I have felt again what parting is: there had been closeness,
but where is it now? Can I feel it still –
how the wonder of closeness was shown to us?
Dark and cruel the moment after, feeling us torn apart.

How defenceless I felt then, having to watch
what had been calling me now letting me go;
yet something stayed, as if all womankind,
small and white, though nothing more

than a wave of the hand, no longer
meant for me – just a wave, no words, as brief
as a flowering plum tree in Spring
from which a cuckoo was called away.

33. Der Apfelgarten
   (1907, Borgeby-Gård)

Komm gleich nach dem Sonnenuntergange,
sieh das Abendgrün des Rasengrunds;
ist es nicht, als hätten wir es lange
angesammelt und erspart in uns,

um es jetzt aus Fühlen und Erinnern,
neuer Hoffnung, halbvergessnem Freun,
noch vermischt mit Dunkel aus dem Innern,
in Gedanken vor uns hinzustreun

unter Bäume wie von Dürer, die
das Gewicht von hundert Arbeitstagen
in den überfüllten Früchten tragen,
dienend, voll Geduld, versuchend, wie

das, was alle Maße übersteigt,
noch zu heben ist und hinzugeben,
wenn man willig, durch ein langes Leben
nur das Eine will und wächst und schweigt.

33. The Apple Orchard
(1907, Borgeby-Gård)

Just after sunset, come and see
the deepening green of the evening lawns,
impressions we long ago received
and saved in us, so that now

that feeling and remembering,
allowing that evening to reappear in front of us –
new hope, and half-forgotten joys
still mixed with the unknown dark inside –

under these trees, like those of Dürer,
trees on which hang the weight
of so much work and care, their heavy fruits
patiently waiting. We try to lift up

what for us surpasses all we know,
and if we are willing, to give it all
through the whole of a long life,
wishing only for one thing: to grow in stillness.

34. Der Duft (1907–8)

Wer bist du, Unbegreiflicher: du Geist,
wie weißt du mich von wo und wann zu finden,
der du das innere (wie Erblinden)
so innig machst, das es sich schließt und kreist.

Der Liebende, der eine an sich reißt,
hat sie nicht nah; nur du allein bist Nähe.
Wen hast du nicht durchtränkt als ob du jähe
Die Farbe seiner Augen seist.

Ach wer Musik in einem Spiegel sähe, der sähe dich und
wüßte, wie du heißt.

34. The Scent (1907–8)

Who are you, spirit beyond my understanding?
How do you know where and when to find me,
to penetrate that which was hidden with such light
that what was fragmented is made whole?

The lover who grasps the beloved to himself
does not bring her near; you alone are nearness.
Is there anyone you have not penetrated
as if suddenly you were the colour of his eyes?

If someone could see music in a mirror,
he would see you, would even know your name.

35. Das Rosen-Innere (1908)

Wo ist zu diesem Innen
ein Außen? Auf welches Weh
legt man solches Linnen?
Welche Himmel spiegeln sich drinnen
in dem Binnensee
dieser offenen Rosen,
dieser sorglosen, sieh:
wie sie lose im Losen
liegen, als könnte nie
eine zitternde Hand sie verschütten.

Sie können sich selber kaum
halten; viele ließen
sich überfüllen und fließen
über von Innenraum
in die Tage, die immer
voller und voller sich schließen,
bis der ganze Sommer ein Zimmer
wird, ein Zimmer in einem Traum.

35. The Rose's Inner Space (1908)

To this inner, where is there an outer?
On what grief does one lay such balm?
What skies are reflected within,
in the lake of these open, carefree roses?
Look how they lie, at ease in their looseness
as though no trembling hand
could ever make them fall.

They cannot really hold themselves
and may let themselves be overfilled,
to flow from their inner space
out into the days that fill, and fuller still
they close themselves until
the whole of summer becomes
just a room within a dream.

36. Die Liebende (1908)

Das ist mein Fenster. Eben
bin ich so sanft erwacht.
Ich dachte, ich würde schweben.
Bis wohin reicht mein Leben,
und wo beginnt die Nacht?

Ich könnte meinen, alles
wäre noch Ich ringsum;
durchsichtig wie eines Kristalles
Tiefe, verdunkelt, stumm.

Ich könnte auch noch die Sterne
fassen in mir; so groß
scheint mir mein Herz; so gerne
ließ es ihn wieder los

den ich vielleicht zu lieben,
vielleicht zu halten begann.
Fremd, wie niebeschrieben
sieht mich mein Schiksal an.

Was bin ich unter diese
Unendlichkeit gelegt,

36. The Beloved (1908)

This is my window.
Just now I awoke so gently
I thought I was floating.
How far does my life extend,
and where does night begin?

I could believe
that everything around me
was still I, transparent
as a crystal's depth
where darkness and silence are ...

I could take hold of the stars
inside me, so great my heart
now seems – so much
it wants to let go of the one

whom perhaps I began
to love, perhaps to hold.
How strange – I don't know how to say it –
the way my destiny looks at me.

duftend wie eine Wiese,
hin und her bewegt,

rufend zugleich und bange,
daß einer den Ruf vernimmt,
und zum Untergange
in einem Andern bestimmt.

How I am lain under this infinity,
fragrant as a meadow,
moved this way and that,

calling, yet fearful
that someone hears the call,
destined to fall completely into another.

37. Die Liebenden (1908)

Sieh, wie sie zueinander erwachsen:
in ihren Adern wird alles Geist.
Ihre Gestalten beben wie Achsen,
um die es heiß und hinreißend kreist.
Dürstende, und sie bekommen zu trinken,
Wache und sieh : sie bekommen zu sehn.
Laß sie ineinander sinken,
um einander zu überstehn.

37. The Lovers (1908)

Look how they awake to each other –
in their veins all becomes spirit,
their trembling forms the axes around which
aroused and enraptured, all is circling.
Thirsty, they are given to drink.
Awake and looking: they are given to see.
Let them sink into each other
so that each may pass beyond.

38. Ich geh jetzt immer den gleichen Pfad (1909)

Ich geh jetzt immer den gleichen Pfad:
am Garten entlang, wo die Rosen grad
Einem sich vorbereiten;
aber ich fühle: noch lang, noch lang
ist das alles nicht mein Empfang,
und ich muss ohne Dank und Klang
ihnen vorüberschreiten.

Ich bin nur der, der den Zug beginnt,
dem die Gaben nicht galten;
bis die kommen, die seliger sind,
lichte, stille Gestalten, –
werden sich alle Rosen im Wind
wie rote Fahnen entfalten.

38. I always take the same path (1909)

I always take the same path
down the garden where the roses
are preparing themselves for us;
but still, long afterwards, I feel
the absence of real greeting –
having to pass them by without thanks,
without meeting.

I am the one who begins a journey
but lacks the quality to sustain it;
when more blessed ones come –
those light, silent figures –
then all the roses will unfold,
red banners in the wind.

39. Von lauter Lauschen ... (1909)

Vor lauter Lauschen und Staunen sei still,
du mein tieftiefes Leben;
dass du weisst, was der Wind dir will,
eh noch die Birken beben.

Und wenn dir einmal das Schweigen sprach,
lass deine Sinne besiegen.
Jedem Hauche gieb dich, gieb nach,
er wird dich lieben und wiegen.

Und dann meine Seele sei weit, sei weit,
dass dir das Leben gelinge,
breite dich wie ein Feierkleid
über die sinnenden Dinge.

39. From wonder and from listening ...
(1909)

From wonder and from listening, be still,
my deepest life, and know
what the wind is bringing
even before the poplars tremble.

When the silence has spoken,
allow your senses to surrender,
give yourself to every breath, give in;
it will cradle you with love.

My soul, be so stretched and so extended,
heart open to embrace all feeling things
that I may truly live.

40. Wenn die Uhren so nah (1909)

Wenn die Uhren so nah
wie im eigenen Herzen schlagen,
und die Dinge mit zagen
Stimmen sich fragen:
Bist du da? – :

Dann bin ich nicht der, der am Morgen erwacht,
einen Namen schenkt mir die Nacht,
den keiner, den ich am Tage sprach,
ohne tiefes Fürchten erführe –

Jede Türe
in mir gibt nach ...

Und da weiß ich, daß nichts vergeht,
keine Geste und kein Gebet
(dazu sind die Dinge zu schwer) –
meine ganze Kindheit steht
immer um mich her.
Niemals bin ich allein.
Viele, die vor mir lebten
und fort von mir strebten,

40. When the clocks strike (1909)

When the clocks strike
as though it were the beating of my heart,
all things saying, voices asking:
Are you there?

Then I am not the one who wakes in the morning;
night gives me a name
which no one I speak to by day
would taste without fear.

And inside me, every door gives way ...

Then I know, nothing is lost –
no gesture and no prayers,
for they have too much weight.
My whole childhood is still here,
it is always around me –
I am never alone.
Many who lived before me
and strove to leave me
yet wove, wove
onto my being.

webten,
webten
an meinem Sein.

Und setz ich mich zu dir her
und sage dir leise: Ich litt –
hörst du?

Wer weiß wer
murmelt es mit.

And if I now sit down beside you
and quietly say: *I suffered* –
do you hear?

Who knows
who is murmuring it too.

41. Lange mußt du leiden ... (1913)

Lange mußt du leiden, kennend nicht was,
bis plötzlich aus gehässig erbissener Frucht
deines Leidens Geschmack eintritt in dir.
Und da liebst du schon fast das Gekostete Keiner
redet dirs wieder aus.

41. Long must you suffer ... (1913)

Long must you suffer, not knowing why,
until out of your suffering's bitter, hateful fruit
the taste suddenly enters into you
and already then, you almost love it.
No one can rob you of it now.

42. Unwissend vor dem Himmel ... (1913)

Unwissend vor dem Himmel meines Lebens,
anstaunend steh ich. O die großen Sterne.
Aufgehendes und Niederstieg. Wie still.
Als wär ich nicht. Nehm ich denn Teil? Entriet ich
dem reinen Einfluss? Wechselt Flut und Ebbe
in meinem Blut nach dieser Ordnung? Abtun
will ich die Wünsche, jeden andern Anschluss,
mein Herz gewöhnen an sein Fernstes. Besser
es lebt im Schrecken seiner Sterne, als
zum Schein beschützt, von einer Näh beschwichtigt.

42. Unknowing in front of the Highest ...
(1913)

Unknowing in front of the Highest in my life,
I stand astonished. Oh, great stars –
the rising, the falling. How still ...
as if I myself were not. Am I taking part?
Did I turn away from that pure influence?
Do the ebb and flow of my own blood
change according to that order?
I shall put aside all my desires and attachments
to attune my heart to its most inner space.

Better to live in terror of distant stars,
than apparently protected
and appeased by what seems near.

43. „Man muss sterben weil man sie kennt." (1913)

*(Papyrus Prisse. Aus den Sprüchen des Ptah-hotep,
Handschrift um 2000 V. CH.)*

„Man muss sterben weil man sie kennt." Sterben
an der unsäglichen Blüte des Lächelns. Sterben
an ihren leichten Händen. Sterben
an Frauen.

Singe der Jüngling die tödlichen,
wenn sie ihm hoch durch den Herzraum
wandeln. Aus seiner blühenden Brust
sing er sie an:
unerreichbare! Ach, wie sie fremd sind.
Über den Gipfeln
seines Gefühls gehn sie hervor und ergießen
süß verwandelte Nacht ins verlassene
Tal seiner Arme. Es rauscht
Wind ihres Aufgangs im Laub seines Leibes. Es glänzen
seine Bäche dahin.

Aber der Mann
schweige erschütterter. Er, der
pfadlos die Nacht im Gebirg

43. "One must die because one knows them." (1913)

(The Prisse Papyrus, from the Maxims of Ptahhotep, *manuscript c. 2000 BC.)*

"One must die because one knows them."
Die from a flowering of smiles we cannot
describe. Die from their delicate hands.
Die from women.

Let the youth sing of those deadly ones –
unreachable ones!

How strange they are.
Above the peaks of his feeling
when they transform him through the passion rising in
    his heart;
then from his flowering breast
he sings to them:
they go forth and pour a sweet night
into the abandoned valley of his arms.
Wind rustles as they rise from the foliage of his body,
where his streams are shining.
He remains silent, shattered,
in his night, pathless

seiner Gefühle geirrt hat:
schweige.

Wie der Seemann schweigt, der ältere,
und die bestandenen
Schrecken spielen in ihm wie in zitternden Käfigen.

in the mountains of his feelings,
he's lost his way; stayed silent.

Just as the sailor, the elder one, stays silent,
and the terrors he endured
play in him as in trembling cages.

44. **Es winkt zu Fühlung ...** (1914)

Es winkt zu Fühlung fast aus allen Dingen,
aus jeder Wendung weht es her: Gedenk!
Ein Tag, an dem wir fremd vorübergingen
entschließt im künftigen sich zum Geschenk.

Wer rechnet unseren Ertrag? Wer trennt
uns von den alten, den vergangnen Jahren?
Was haben wir seit Anbeginn erfahren,
Als daß sich eins im anderen erkennt?

Als daß an uns gleichgültiges erwarmt?
O Haus, o Wiesenhang, o Abendlicht,
auf einmal bringst du's beinah zum Gesicht
und stehst an uns, umarmend und umarmt.

Durch alle Wesen reicht der eine Raum:
Weltinnenraum. Die Vögel fliegen still
durch uns hindurch. O, der ich wachsen will,
ich seh hinaus, und in mir wächst der Baum.

Ich sorge mich, und in mir steht das Haus.
Ich hüte mich, und in mir ist die Hut.
Geliebter, der ich wurde: an mir ruht
der schönen Schöpfung Bild und weint sich aus.

44. **All things beckon us to feel ...** (1914)

All things beckon us to feel, to be related;
we are called at every turn: *remember*.
We will be shown that a day
we passed by, like strangers, was a gift.

Who works out what is our due? Who frees us
from the weary years that pass?
From our beginning, what have we learned
except that in another, I may recognise myself,

that indifference has warmed itself from us?
Oh, house, hillside meadow, twilight,
suddenly you almost bring it into view
and stand by us, embracing and embraced.

One space reaches through all beings:
world-inner-space. Birds fly right through us,
silently. I wish to grow from that, I look
outwards, but *inside* me there grows the tree.

I am anxious, and in me stands the house;
I am on my guard, and in me there is care.
Beloved, whom I became: close to me there is still
the image of a fine creation; it weeps and weeps.

45. Ausgesetzt auf den Bergen des Herzens ... (1914)

Ausgesetzt auf den Bergen des Herzens.
Siehe, wie klein dort,
siehe: die letzte Ortschaft der Worte, und höher,
aber wie klein auch, noch ein letztes
Gehöft von Gefühl. Erkennst du's?
Ausgesetzt auf den Bergen des Herzens. Steingrund
unter den Händen. Hier blüht wohl einiges auf;
aus stummem Absturz
blüht ein unwissendes Kraut singend hervor.
Aber der Wissende? Ach, der zu wissen begann
und schweigt nun, ausgesetzt auf den Bergen
des Herzens.
Da geht wohl, heilen Bewußtseins,
manches umher, manches gesicherte Bergtier,
wechselt und weilt. Und der große geborgene Vogel
kreist um der Gipfel reine Verweigerung. – Aber
ungeborgen, hier auf den Bergen des Herzens ...

45. Abandoned on the mountains of the heart (1914)

Abandoned on the mountains of the heart.
See, how small there – see, the last village of words,
and higher, but how small as well, a last farmstead yet
of feeling. Do you recognise it?
Abandoned on the mountains of the heart. Rock
under hands. Here, opening and flowering
may well take place; from a still precipice
there emerges to flower a singing, unknowing herb.
But the one who knows? Oh, he who began to know
is silent now, abandoned on the mountains of the heart.

Out of healing consciousness one senses
things are wandering about:
some protecting mountain creature
changes and stays. And the huge hidden bird
circles around the peak of pure denial … but
here, not hidden … on the mountains of the heart.

46. Liebesanfang (1915)

O Lächeln, erstes Lächeln, unser Lächeln.
Wie war das Eines: Duft der Linden atmen,
Parkstille hören – , plötzlich in einander
aufschaun und staunen bis heran ans Lächeln.

In diesem Lächeln war Erinnerung
an einen Hasen, der da eben drüben
im Rasen spielte; dieses war die Kindheit
des Lächelns. Ernster schon war ihm des Schwanes
Bewegung eingegeben, den wir später
den Weiher teilen sahen in zwei Hälften
lautlosen Abends. – Und der Wipfel Ränder
gegen den reinen, freien, ganz schon künftig
nächtigen Himmel hatten diesem Lächeln
Ränder gezogen gegen die entzückte
Zukunft im Antlitz.

46. Love's Beginning (1915)

Smiles, the first ones – our smiles. Such a moment:
breathing the scent of the lime trees, hearing
the stillness of the park; the sudden wonder
of seeing each other … turned into smiles.

In this smiling there was the memory
of a hare that played in the grass:
smiling's childhood. Deeper the impression
of the movement of the swan we saw
in the silent evening
dividing that little pond into two halves.
And already the outline of the treetops
set against the pure, clear, soon-to-be night sky
is like a boundary to this smiling
in the face of future delight.

47. **Wunderliches Wort** (1919)

Wunderliches Wort: *die Zeit vertreiben*!
Sie zu *halten*, wäre das Problem.
Denn, wen ängstigts nicht: wo ist ein Bleiben,
wo ein endlich *Sein* in alledem? –

Sieh, der Tag verlangsamt sich, entgegen
jenem Raum, der ihn nach Abend nimmt:
Aufstehn wurde Stehn, und Stehn wird Legen,
und das willig Liegende verschwimmt –

Berge ruhn, von Sternen überprächtigt; –
aber auch in ihnen flimmert Zeit.
Ach, in meinem wilden Herzen nächtigt
obdachlos die Unvergänglichkeit.

47. **Strange saying** (1919)

Strange saying: *to pass the time*!
Holding it is what's so hard.
Who awakes to wonder, is it possible
to stay? And where in the midst of
everything can one *be*?

Do you see, the day slows down towards
a space that takes it into evening;
rising turns into standing, into lying down,
the willingly supine, vague and actually ... asleep.

Mountains rest but the stars surpass them,
and even in them, remorseless time
runs on. Yet that which is homeless and everlasting,
shelters in my wild heart ...

48. O sage, Dichter ... (1921)

O sage, Dichter, was du tust?

                    Ich rühme.

Aber das Tödliche und Ungetüme,
wie haltst du's aus, wie nimmst du's hin?

                    Ich rühme.

Aber das Namenlose, Anonyme,
wie rufst du's, Dichter, dennoch an?

                    Ich rühme.

Woher dein Recht, in jeglichem Kostüme,
in jeder Maske wahr zu sein?

                    Ich rühme.

Und daß das Stille und das Ungestüme
wie Stern und Sturm dich kennen?:

                    Weil ich rühme.

48. Poet, tell us ... (1921)

Poet, tell us what you do.

> I praise.

But the deadly, the monstrous –
how do you bear them, allow them in?

> I praise.

How is it that the nameless, the unknown
nevertheless can call you?

> I praise.

What right have you in any role,
in any mask, to remain free and true inside?

> I praise.

And that both chaos and stillness know you
as well they know storm and stars?

> Because I praise.

49. *Die Sonette an Orpheus I–1*: **Da stieg ein Baum ...** (1922)

Da stieg ein Baum. O reine Übersteigung!
O Orpheus singt! O hoher Baum im Ohr!
Und alles schwieg. Doch selbst in der Verschweigung
ging neuer Anfang, Wink und Wandlung vor.

Tiere aus Stille drangen aus dem klaren
gelösten Wald von Lager und Genist;
und da ergab sich, daß sie nicht aus List
und nicht aus Angst in sich so leise waren,

sondern aus Hören. Brüllen, Schrei, Geröhr
schien klein in ihren Herzen. Und wo eben
kaum eine Hütte war, dies zu empfangen,

ein Unterschlupf aus dunkelstem Verlangen
mit einem Zugang, dessen Pfosten beben, –
da schufst du ihnen Tempel im Gehör.

49. *The Sonnets to Orpheus I–1*: There stands a tree ... (1922)

There stands a tree, an axis high and pure –
Orpheus sings! O soaring tree, which now I hear!
And all was silent. Yet in that refrain from speech
a new beginning came, a sign, and change.

It freed the forest: out of the silence,
out of their hides and lairs, the animals appeared,
and one could sense it was not from fear
or cunning that they were so quiet,

but from listening: shouting, yelling or baying
then were felt as petty in their hearts.
Where there had been no place open to receive,

from their deepest longing you created a refuge
at whose entrance the posts were trembling:
a temple in their listening.

50. *Die Sonette an Orpheus II–27*: Gibt es wirklich ... (1922)

Gibt es wirklich die Zeit, die zerstörende?
Wann, auf dem ruhenden Berg, zerbricht sie die Burg?
Dieses Herz, das unendlich den Göttern gehörende,
wann vergewaltigts der Demiurg?

Sind wir wirklich so ängstlich Zerbrechliche,
wie das Schicksal uns wahr machen will?
Ist die Kindheit, die tiefe versprechliche,
in den Wurzeln – später – still?

Ach, das Gespenst des Vergänglichen,
durch den arglos Empfänglichen
geht es, als wär es ein Rauch.

Als die, die wir sind, als die Treibenden,
gelten wir doch bei bleibenden
Kräften als göttlicher Brauch.

50. *The Sonnets to Orpheus II–27*: Time the Destroyer (1922)

Does time the destroyer really exist?
When will it destroy the fortress on the
    peaceful mountain?
When will this heart – which is the gods' in all eternity –
be violated by the lower forces?

Are we really so anxiously fragile
as Fate would have us believe?
Is childhood, with its promise and depth,
in its roots, later to be silenced?

The dread of being transient
is like a haunting fragrance
in all we unknowingly receive.

But we, who we are, must strive,
recognised by the eternal powers
as the means of fulfilment.

51. Sonett

O das Neue, Freunde, ist nicht dies,
dass Maschinen uns die Hand verdrängen.
Lasst euch nicht beirrn von Übergängen,
bald wird schweigen, wer das „Neue" pries.

Denn das Ganze ist unendlich neuer,
als ein Kabel und ein hohes Haus.
Seht die Sterne sind ein altes Feuer,
und die neuern Feuer löschen aus.

Glaubt nicht, dass die längsten Transmissionen
schon des Künftigen Räder drehn.
Denn Aeonen reden mit Aeonen.

Mehr, als wir erfuhren, ist geschehen.
Und die Zukunft fasst das Allerfernste
rein in eins mit unserm innern Ernste.

51. Sonnet

My friends, it is not that our hands are pushed aside
by these machines that is really new.
Don't let yourselves be fooled by change –
the one who praises progress will soon be dumb.

Wholeness is endlessly new
in a way in which no skyscraper or electrical device
    can ever be.
See the stars, still alive with an ancient fire,
and the latest fires all will die.

Don't believe the newest transmissions
are already driving the future's wheels –
for Aeons only speak with Aeons.

More has taken place than we have experienced.
The future holds what is most distant,
holds it pure, at one with our innermost being.

52. Imaginärer Lebenslauf (1923)

Erst eine Kindheit, grenzenlos und ohne
Verzicht und Ziel. O unbewußte Lust.
Auf einmal Schrecken, Schranke, Schule, Frohne
und Absturz in Versuchung und Verlust.

Trotz. Der Gebogene wird selber Bieger
und rächt an anderen, daß er erlag.
Geliebt, gefürchtet, Retter, Ringer, Sieger
und Überwinder, Schlag auf Schlag.

Und dann allein im Weiten, Leichten, Kalten.
Doch tief in der errichteten Gestalt
ein Atemholen nach dem Ersten, Alten ...
Da stürzte Gott aus seinem Hinterhalt.

52. An Imagined Life (1923)

It seemed a childhood without limits did begin –
no holding back, or even any aim. Unconscious desire.
But suddenly: terror, barriers, school, drudgery,
precipitous fall into temptation, loss.

Defiance. The bullied one becomes a bully,
bent on revenge for the hurt endured.
Loved, feared, saviour, warrior, victor,
conqueror, blow on blow.

Then, alone in space, in distance, in lightness, cold.
Yet in the form that there was made
a deep breath is moving towards
the very beginning, old.

And plunging from his ambush, God.

53. Wir sind nur Mund (1923)

Wir sind nur Mund.
Wer singt das ferne Herz,
das heil inmitten aller Dinge weilt?
Sein großer Schlag ist in uns eingeteilt
in kleine Schläge. Und sein großer Schmerz
ist, wie sein großer Jubel, uns zu groß.

So reißen wir uns immer wieder los
und sind nur Mund. Aber auf einmal bricht
der große Herzschlag in uns ein,
so daß wir schrein –,
und sind dann Wesen, Wandlung und Gesicht.

53. Are we mute? (1923)

Are we mute? Who sings of the distant heart
That remains intact within all things?
In us his great ringing sound is divided
into tiny ones. For us, his great sorrow
and great joy are both too big.

Again and again we tear ourselves away,
stay dumb. Then suddenly
the ringing of the great heart breaks in on us,
we cry out ... then we experience
being, transformation, vision.

54. Schweigen (1924)

Für Frau Fanette Clavel

Schweigen. Wer inneger schwieg,
rührt an die Wurzeln der Rede.
Einmal wird ihm dann jede
erwachsene Silbe zum Sieg:

über das, was im Schweigen nicht schweigt,
über das höhnische Böse;
daß es sich spurlos löse,
ward ihm das Wort gezeigt.

54. Staying silent (1924)

For Mrs Fanette Clavel

Saying silent. The one who stays silent
deep inside, touches the root of speech
and one day will master
words that have grown:
master what in silence is not silent,
master scornful evil;
he was shown the word
so that it can vanish
without trace.

55. Spaziergang (1924)

Schon ist mein Blick am Hügel, dem besonnten,
dem Wege, den ich kaum begann, voran.
So faßt uns das, was wir nicht fassen konnten,
voller Erscheinung, aus der Ferne an –

und wandelt uns, auch wenn wirs nicht erreichen,
in jenes, das wir, kaum es ahnend, sind;
ein Zeichen weht, erwidernd unserm Zeichen ...
Wir aber spüren nur den Gegenwind.

55. My Walk (1924)

My walk has only just begun, but my look
is already on that sunny hill far ahead.
So we are taken by what, in splendour,
comes to us from afar; we cannot grasp it

and cannot reach it, yet it changes us
into what, unknowingly, we already are;
there is a breeze, a sign in answer to our sign ...
but we only sense the headwind.

56. Eine Furche in meinem Hirn (1924)

Eine Furche in meinem Hirn,
eine Linie meiner Hand:
hält die Gewohnheit stand,
wird sie mir beides verwirrn.

Rette dich und entflieh
aus dem verengten Netz.
Wirf ein neues Gesetz
über dich und sie.

56. A furrow in my brain (1924)

A furrow in my brain,
a line upon my hand:
as long as I am trapped in habit,
confusion shall prevail.

Save yourself and flee
the narrowed net:
let a different law prevail
over you, and over her.

57. Klang (1925)

Klang, nichtmehr mit Gehör
meßbar. Als wäre der Ton,
der uns rings übertrifft,
eine Reife des Raums.

57. Sound (1925)

A sound my ears cannot measure –
ringing,
surrounding and surpassing us:
the fulfilment of space.

58. Rose, oh reiner Widerspruch (1925)

Rose, oh reiner Widerspruch, Lust,
Niemandes Schlaf zu sein unter soviel Lidern.

58. Rose, oh pure contradiction ... (1925)

Rose, oh pure contradiction, desire,
to be no one's sleep
under so many eyelids.

Translator's note: Rilke chose this poem as his epitaph.

59. Bruder Körper ... (1926)

Für Herrn und Frau Verrijn-Stuart

Bruder Körper is arm ...: da heißt es, reich sein für ihn.
Oft war er der Reiche: so sei ihm verziehn
das Armsein seiner argen Momente.
Wenn er dann tut, als ob er uns kaum noch kennte,
darf man ihn leise erinnern an alles Gemeinsame.

Freilich wir sind nicht Eines, sondern zwei Einsame:
Unser Bewußtsein und Er;
Aber wie vieles, das wir einander weither
verdanken,
wie Freunde es tun! Und man erfährt im Erkranken:
Freunde haben es schwer!

59. Brother body ... (1926)

For Mr and Mrs Verrijn-Stuart

Brother body is poor ... so one must be rich for his sake.
Often *he* was the rich one, so he may be forgiven
the poverty of his difficult moments.
If he now hardly seems to know us anymore,
one may gently remind him of all we have shared.

Of course, we are not one.
There are two of us, both lonely:
our consciousness, and him.
But we are grateful to each other
for so much, as friends are.
And one discovers that, in illness,
for a friend, it is hard!

60. Komm du, du letzter ... (1926)

Komm du, du letzter, den ich anerkenne,
heilloser Schmerz im leiblichen Geweb:
wie ich im Geiste brannte, sieh, ich brenne
in dir; das Holz hat lange widerstrebt,
der Flamme, die du loderst, zuzustimmen,
nun aber nähr' ich dich und brenn in dir.
Mein hiesig Mildsein wird in deinem Grimmen
ein Grimm der Hölle nicht von hier.
Ganz rein, ganz planlos frei von Zukunft stieg
ich auf des Leidens wirren Scheiterhaufen,
so sicher nirgend Künftiges zu kaufen
um dieses Herz, darin der Vorrat schwieg.
Bin ich es noch, der da unkenntlich brennt?
Erinnerungen reiß ich nicht herein.
O Leben, Leben: Draußensein.
Und ich in Lohe. Niemand der mich kennt.

60. Come, you last one ... (1926)

Come, you last one. I recognise you,
incurable pain in the body's web;
as once I burned in the mind, now look, see
how I burn in you; the wood had long refused
to yield to the flame that
you had lit,
but now I feed that fire, and there I burn.
In your grim pain my habitual mildness
must turn into the fury of an alien hell.
In innocence, futureless and free, I climbed
suffering's twisted pyre towards the stake,
certain I could not purchase any future
for this heart, whose reserves were mute.
Is it still I, who am burning unacknowledged?

I do not clutch at memories in this fire.
Oh life, life ... to be outside myself.
And I, aflame. Not known by anyone.

Translator's note: Rilke died ten days after writing this poem. Moreover, the original poem ended with the following four lines, which the poet chose to delete:

(Giving up. It's not like illness was in childhood –
a postponement, an excuse for growing up
when everything called and whispered. But now
is not the place for the wonder I did feel then.)

61. Rilke's Walk with the Old Man: A Poem by the Translator

One day, Rilke joined the old man
on his walk along the river, and asked:
"Why are you looking down?"

"I am half-blind now, uneasy
because of the uneven pavement slabs, and –"

"But the river!" Rilke said. "The river!"

November. The month my father died.
We drove him from the hospital, home to die.
To die; what does this *mean*?

Grey and misty, leaves yellow, wet, then, as now.
He still could walk, speak, remember;
came to the window once to call
my mother to the telephone.
How he had said, in his own way,
that he was ready.

In bed, listening to music he loved,
struggling to find words.

The last night, mother and I at his bedside,
candles at the head, trying to pray,
despairing, suddenly quiet,
then, for the first time,
completely silent: waiting.
Waiting?

Each breath shallower than the last.
Then, silence. We were all silent.
They call it *death* ... but nothing had changed,
except for one thing – his face relaxed; relaxed completely.
Extraordinary, beautiful.
Whose face was that?

The old man looked up. Blue sky.
The sun was even warm, the wide tidal river
shining back to Heaven, saying:

"This is my response: you are there, I am here;
now there is light, but I know that when it's grey
and I am sullen and morose, you are still there,
maintaining all."

Can I remember, remember to reply?
My little voice is much less important than I think –
but it is needed, too.

About the Translator

Tilo Ulbricht was born in Germany in 1928 and immigrated to England with his parents. He has written poetry since the age of nine, but made no attempt to publish them for decades, as they were intensely personal.

In later life he was a member of the West London Poetry Circle, which met at his house regularly. The group held several recitals at a gallery in Kensington, and published its poems in booklets.

He is the author of the play *Heresy*, directed at the Tabard Theatre, London, in 2014.

For several years, he was the London editor of the magazine *Parabola*, in which his article about Rilke, "A Thousand Roots", appeared.

Feeling Rilke to be a fellow spirit, but encountering one disappointing translation after another, he began to translate Rilke himself. He spent four years translating *The Duino Elegies*, and, later, many of Rilke's shorter poems, some of which were published by the Internet magazine *in-between*.

Selected Titles from Paper + Ink

I Cleaned the – & Other Stories:
Winners of the Commonwealth Short Story Prize 2021

The Great Indian Tee and Snakes & Other Stories:
Winners of the Commonwealth Short Story Prize 2020

Emissaries: Stories and Reflections
Dean William Rudoy

In Dreams: The Very Short Works of Ryūnosuke Akutagawa
Selected and Translated from the Japanese by Ryan Choi

Million-Story City: The Undiscovered Writings of Marcus Preece
Edited by Malu Halasa and Aura Saxén

Another Man
Leslie Croxford

The Dead
James Joyce

The Overcoat
Nikolai Gogol
Translated from the Russian by Constance Garnett

Bartleby, the Scrivener
Herman Melville

Independence Day & Other Stories
Pramoedya Ananta Toer
Translated from the Indonesian by Willem Samuels

In the Shadow of Death
Rūdolfs Blaumanis
Translated from the Latvian by Uldis Balodis

The Necklace & Other Stories
Guy de Maupassant

www.paperand.ink